Bone Appétit

The following Internet sites have been kind enough to take recipes from this book and place them online in special sections which will feature new recipes every month! Be sure to check them out!

Many thanks to Mike Jennett & his Internet site "Dogs By The Bay"

www.dogsbythebay.com

Also, many thanks to Top Dog Endeavors

www.tdog.com

Begin your search for anything in the Dog World with Top Dog Endeavors. Over 2C hundred pages all dedicated to dogs, dog products and dog services.

Nation's BEST Animal Newspaper:

www.californiamedia.com

Special thanks to:

My family
for all their help and support

Mike Jennett (Dogs by the Bay)
for his gracious support and marketing help with this book

Christine & Erin (*P.A.W.S.*)
for their ongoing dedication and drive supporting the AIDS community and their pets

Heidi Kistler (the Pawsitively Pampered Pet)
for being such a wonderfully positive, happy and inspirational dog lover

Nina (Waggers)
for allowing me to test the very first copies of this book

Betty Estes (Westco Graphics, Inc.)
for our shared enthusiasm of our puppy pals and her professional support

Vic Spain, D.V.M.
for taking so much time editing and helping me with this book

Kristine Gonzales, D.V.M.
for graciously contributing her expertise to make this book possible

Llana Strubel, D.V.M.
for caring enough to work with PAWS and help with this book

Judie Gerber, D.V.M.
for generously offering editorial help and professional expertise with this book

and of course the animals:
Günther, Max, Freeway, Scruffy, Poppy, Baron, Bogie, Annie, Snuggie, Angel, Noodles the Poodle (Australia), Hazel, Barley, Dobie, Cuddles, Ms. Piggy, Gingus, Peppy and Xerox.

Bone Appétit

"the world's finest dog biscuit recipe cookbook"

by Branko E. Romano

This book has been manufactured and assembled by the employees of A.R.C. (Association of Retarded Citizens). With this purchase you have helped others, and we thank you.

• • •

Also, proceeds from the sales of this book go toward animal shelters in need of funds. With this purchase, you have helped needy animals. And for this, too, we thank you.

This book has been reviewed, edited & approved by:

Vic Spain, D.V.M., Medical Chief of Staff
S.F. SPCA Animal Hospital • U.C. Davis class of '93

Kristine Gonzales, D.V.M.
S.F. SPCA Animal Hospitai • U.C. Davis class of '93

Llana Strubel, D.V.M.
S.F. SPCA Animal Hospital • University of Illinois class of '95

Judie Gerber, D.V.M.
S.F. SPCA Animal Hospital • Ontario Veterinary College, University of Guelph class of '89

Note: Commentary at the bottom of each recipe page is intended for entertainment purposes only!

This book is available at high discounts for fundraising purposes and volume purchases

...please contact the publisher (1-800-550-BOOK).
Thank you for your interest and support.

Published By:

California Media

a division of West Coast Media Group, Inc.

P.O. Box 8245 • Emeryville • California • 94662

Toll-Free: 1-800-550-BOOK

tel: 510-655-8036 • fax: 510-601-6938

Email: boneappetit@californiamedia.com

www.californiamedia.com

•

Web Page Design, Graphic Design, Recipes & Layout by:

California Media & Branko E. Romano

•

Library of Congress Cataloging-in-Publication Data

Romano, Branko E., 1969-
Bone appétit : the world's finest dog biscuit recipe cookbook / by Branko E. Romano.
p. cm.
ISBN 1-890613-01-0 (alk. paper)
1. Dogs--Food--Recipes. 2. Dogs--Quotations, maxims, etc.
I. Title.
SF427.4.R65 1998 97-51401
636.7'0855--dc21 CIP

"A Dog's Prayer"

"Treat me kindly, my beloved master, for no heart in all the world is more grateful for kindness than the loving heart of me. Do not break my spirit with a stick, for though I should lick your hand between blows, your patience and understanding will more quickly teach me the things you would have me do. Speak to me often, for your voice is the world's sweetest music, as you must know by the fierce wagging of my tail when your footstep falls upon my waiting ear. When it is cold and wet, please take me inside, for I am now a domesticated animal, no longer used to bitter elements. And I ask no greater glory than the privilege of sitting at your feet beside the hearth. Though had you no home, I would rather follow you through ice and snow than rest upon the softest pillow in the warmest home in all the land, for you are my god and I am your devoted worshipper. Keep my pan filled with fresh water, for although I should not reproach you were it dry, I cannot tell you when I suffer thirst. Feed me clean food, that I may stay well, to romp and play and do your bidding, to walk by your side, and stand ready, willing and able to protect you with my life should your life be in danger. And, beloved master, should the great Master see fit to deprive me of my health or sight, do not turn me away from you. Rather hold me gently in your arms as skilled hands grant me the merciful boon of eternal rest --- and I will leave you knowing with the last breath I drew, my fate was ever safest in your hands."

\- Beth Norman Harris

Table of Contents

Table of Contents

A Note From The Vet:

1. Biscuits should not take the place of a well-balanced dog food.

2. Biscuits should only be fed in small quantities, particularly with puppies or dogs not used to having biscuits.

3. If your dog has any allergies to food products, please make sure you eliminate them from any recipes in which they appear. If you are ever in doubt, or have any questions about any of the recipes contained within, please consult your veterinarian.

Health Information:

This is a list of ingredients that have the potential to cause problems for dogs prone to food allergies, pancreatic disorders, or who even just have "sensitive" intestinal tracts. If you are concerned, please consult your veterinarian prior to giving your dog any new food.

- Wheat flour / wheat germ / cracked wheat
- Dairy products; particularly butter, milk & cream (high in fat and sometimes causes diarrhea)
- Onions (has the potential to cause anemia)
- Bacon bits, bacon fat, shortening, coconut oil & tuna oil (high in fat)
- Gravy (high in fat)
- Liverwurst / sausage (high in fat)
- Peanut butter (high in fat)

The recipes which contain these ingredients only call for small quantities, so they are unlikely to cause problems. Please be sure to only feed your dog one to two biscuits as a treat. Never replace a well-balanced dogfood with biscuits, it could cause serious health problems.

Health Chart:

The ***health chart*** on the following page lists most of the ingredients you will find in this book. For diet-conscious dogs (and the people they own) refer to this chart when determining the approximate nutritional value of any biscuit.

HEALTH CHART

Description	Amount	Fat (Grams)	Saturated Fat (Grams)	Calories (Kc)	Cholesterol (Mg)
Almonds (Slivered)	1 Cup	70	6.7	795	0
Baking Powder	1 tsp	0	0	5	0
Bananas	1 Ban.	1	.2	105	0
Barbecue Sauce	1 Tbsp	0	0	10	0
Beef Broth (Bouillon)	1 Cup	1	.3	15	0
Beef Chuck (Lean)	2.8 Oz	8	2.7	175	75
Bouillon (Dry)	1 Pkt	1	.3	15	1
Broccoli	1 Cup	0	.1	45	0
Brown Gravy	1 Cup	2	.9	80	2
Buckwheat Flour	1 Cup	1	.2	340	0
Bulgur	1 Cup	3	.2	600	0
Butter (Unsalted)	1 Tbsp	11	7.1	100	31
Carrots (Cooked)	1 Cup	0	.1	70	0
Cheddar Cheese	1 Oz	9	6	115	30
Coconut (Shredded)	1 Cup	27	23.8	285	0
Corn Oil	1 Tbsp	14	1.8	125	0
Cornmeal	1 Cup	4	.5	440	0
Eggs	1 Egg	5	1.6	75	213
Garlic Powder	1 tsp	0	0	10	0
Margarine	1 Tbsp	9	1.8	75	0
Milk (lowfat)	1 Cup	5	2.9	120	18
Milk (skim)	1 Cup	0	.3	85	4
Milk (whole)	1 Cup	8	5.1	150	33
Molasses	2 Tbsp	0	0	85	0
Nonfat Dry Milk	1 Envlpe	1	.4	325	17
Oregano	1 tsp	0	0	5	0
Peanut Butter	1 Tbsp	8	1.4	95	0
Pineapple Juice	1 Cup	0	0	140	0
Safflower Oil	1 Tbsp	14	1.3	125	0
Sugar (granulated)	1 Tbsp	0	0	45	0
Syrup (corn & maple)	2 Tbsp	0	0	122	0
Vegetable Shortening	1 Tbsp	13	3.3	115	0
Wheat Flour	1 Cup	1	.2	455	0
Whole-wheat Flour	1 Cup	2	.3	400	0
Yeast Dry, Active	1 Pkg	0	0	20	0

"Outside of a dog, a book is man's best friend. Inside of a dog it's too dark to read."

- Groucho Marx

Trivia Time...

A fully grown 2 year old Yorkie was 2 1/2 inches tall by 3 3/4 inches long. Weighing 4 ounces.

Actual Size:

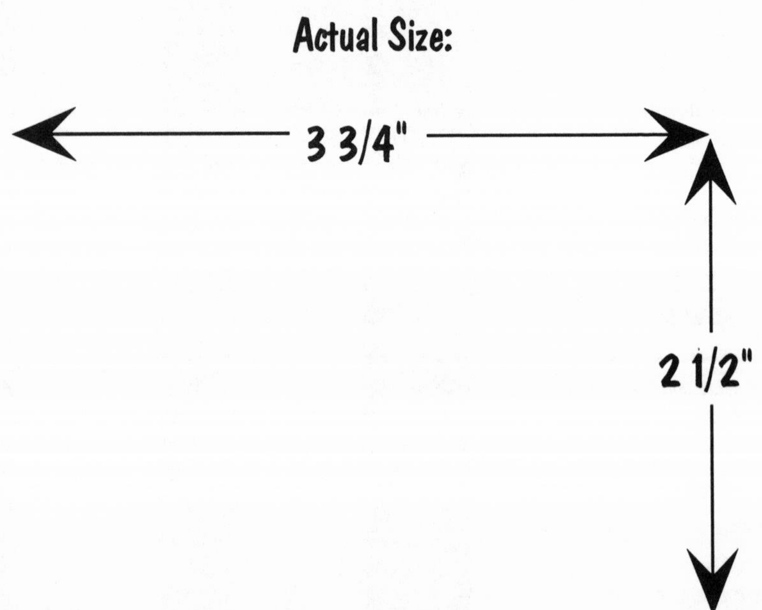

CHEDDAR CHEESE BISCUIT BAKES

1 1/2 c. whole wheat flour
1 1/4 c. grated cheddar cheese
1/4 c. corn oil margarine
1 clove garlic, minced
1/8 tsp. salt
Nonfat Milk

Preheat oven to 375 degrees.
Leave the cheese in a bowl
until it is room temperature.
Blend the cheese with the softened
margarine, garlic, salt and flour.
Knead into a ball (use as much milk as needed).
Refrigerate for 30 minutes.
Place mixture on a floured surface
and roll out. Cut into little biscuits.
Bake for 15 minutes or until brown.

Makes 36 biscuits

Makes a nice side dish!

"You think dogs will not be in heaven? I tell you, they will be there long before any of us."

- Robert Louis Stevenson

Trivia Time...

More than 6 in 10 pet owners have a dog.

POOCH'S PROZAK KRUNCHIES

undepressingly delicious

2 c. whole wheat flour
2/3 c. yellow cornmeal
1/2 c. sunflower seeds, shelled
dash of salt
pinch of sugar
2 tbsp. corn oil
1/2 c. chicken broth
2 eggs, mixed with 1/4 c. milk
1 egg, beaten

Preheat oven to 350 degrees.
In a large bowl, blend together flour, cornmeal, sugar, salt and seeds.
Add oil, chicken broth and egg/milk mixture.
Let sit 30 minutes.
Place mixture on floured surface.
Roll out dough 1/4 inch thick.
Cut into small circles, shape like smiley faces, and brush with beaten egg.
Bake 30 minutes, until golden brown.
Let stand until cool.

Makes about 40 treats

Provides frantic tail wagging on those rainy days!

"Scratch a dog and you'll find a permanent job."

- Franklin P. Jones

Trivia Time...

Over 36 million homes nationwide have at least one dog.

LOVELY LIVER LICKIES

3/4 c. wheat germ
3/4 c. nonfat dry milk powder
1 egg
1 (3 1/2 oz.) liver-flavored baby food
1 tbsp. bran
1 tbsp. Brewer's yeast

Preheat oven to 350 degrees.
Mix together all the ingredients.
If mixture is dry, add a small amount of water.
Drop by teaspoonfuls on greased cookie sheet.
Bake for 20 minutes.
Let stand on cookie rack until cool.

Makes 18 snacks

A tasty summer treat!

"Whenever hound was heard to whine, They gave the children bread and wine. Whenever hound was heard to bark, They thought the dead walk'd in the dark. Whenever hound was heard to howl, They thought they saw a corpse's cowl."

- Danish Ballad of Svend Dyring

Question:

If dogs eat grass, are they sick?

Answer:

No. Veterinarians do not know why dogs eat grass, but it does not mean that they are sick. *However,* it does mean they like grass.

TERIYAKI TASTIES

2 c. whole wheat flour
3/4 c. yellow cornmeal
3 tbsp. bacon fat
1/4 c. vegetable oil
2 c. all purpose flour

4 beef bouillon cubes
2 c. boiling water
Crisp bacon bits
Teriyaki sauce

Preheat oven to 350 degrees.
Combine first 5 ingredients; mix well.
Dissolve bouillon in boiling water and
add bouillon to mixture. Add bacon bits.
Mix to make dough (stiff).
Roll onto a floured surface. Shape into biscuits.
Bake for 30 minutes. Let stand 24 hours.
When hard, brush each biscuit with teriyaki sauce,
and bake again for 5 minutes at 350 degrees.
Let stand until cool.

Makes 36 biscuits

Garnish with orange wedges!

"Whoever said you can't buy happiness forgot little puppies."
- Gene Hill

Question:
If a dog's nose is hot, is it sick?

Answer:
No. A Kansas State University class studied 75 dogs and determined that the nose doesn't determine anything about the health of the dog.

STEAK FLAVORED BISCUITS

1 c. whole wheat flour
2 tbsp. wheat germ
1/4 c. bran flakes
1/4 c. soy flour
1 tbsp. molasses
2 tbsp. oil or fat
1 tbsp. kelp or 1/2 tsp. salt
1 tsp. sage
1/2 tsp. bone meal
1/3 c. milk or water
Steak sauce

Preheat oven to 350 degrees.
Mix all the ingredients together.
Knead mixture for 3 minutes. Shape into little biscuits.
Bake 30 minutes or until golden brown.
Turn off heat and leave in oven for one hour.
Let stand until cool.
Brush with steak sauce, return to preheated
350 degree oven, and bake for another 7 minutes.

Makes 4 dozen biscuits

"Recollect that the Almighty, who gave the dog to be companion of our pleasures and our toils, hath invested him with a nature noble and incapable of deceit."

- Sir Walter Scott

Question:

Are dogs color blind?

Answer:

No. Dogs can see some colors, but not as well as humans. Different types of dogs tend to see different colors.

FIDO'S TEENY TINY TIDBITS

1 c. rolled oats
1/3 c. margarine
1 c. boiling water
1/2 c. milk
1 c. cheddar cheese (shredded)
3/4 c. cornmeal
1 tbsp. sugar
1 egg, beaten
1-2 tsp. chicken or beef bouillon
2-3 c. whole wheat flour

Preheat oven to 325 degrees. Grease cookie sheets. Combine oats, margarine and water - let stand for 15 minutes. Stir in milk, cheese, cornmeal, sugar, egg and bouillon; mix well. Slowly blend in flour, to form a stiff dough. On a floured surface, knead for 5 minutes. Roll out to 1/2-inch thickness and cut into little pieces. Bake for 40 minutes.

Makes 60 teeny tiny biscuits

Lovely with afternoon tea!

"No man can be condemned for owning a dog. As long as he has a dog, he has a friend; and the poorer he gets, the better friend he has."

- Will Rogers

Trivia Time...

One half of all dog owners purchase a toy or related product for their dog.

MICROWAVED MUNCHIES

1 c. whole wheat flour
1/2 c. all purpose flour
3/4 c. nonfat dry milk powder
1/2 c. quick cooking rolled oats
1/2 c. yellow cornmeal
1/4 tsp. salt
1 tsp. sugar
1 beef bouillon cube
1/2 c. boiling water
1/3 cup shortening
1 egg

In large bowl, mix dry ingredients.
Mix in shortening until crumbly, then add egg.
Dissolve 1 bouillon cube in 1/2 cup hot water.
Mix bouillon water with dry mixture.
On floured surface, knead for 3 minutes.
Roll into 1/2 inch thick sheet. Cut into biscuits.
Microwave on full power until hard (about 7 minutes).
Be sure to flip the biscuits over during cooking time.

Makes 36 biscuits

A wonderful treat for the bow-wow on the go!

"Ever consider what they must think of us? I mean, here we come back from a grocery store with the most amazing haul- chicken, pork, half a cow... they must think we're the greatest hunters on earth!"

- Anne Tyler

* MUNCHIE PAWS

A recipe dedicated to the organization of PAWS (Pets Are Wonderful Support) of San Francisco, California.

"PAWS is a community based non-profit organization dedicated to helping improve the quality of life for people with AIDS by enabling them to keep their companion animals with them for as long as possible. Equally important, we serve as an advocate for the health and well being of all companion animals under our care. In addition, PAWS educates the medical community, and community at large about the special risks associated with zoonotic diseases."

PAWS, San Francisco
Tel: 415-241-1460
Fax: 415-252-9471

Look in your local phone directory for the PAWS organization near you.

*MUNCHIE PAWS

dedicated to Pets Are Wonderful Support

2 sm. jars strained baby beef
Dash of sugar
1/4 c. nonfat dry milk powder
1/4 tsp. salt
1/2 c. wheat germ
Healthy dash of love

Preheat oven to 325 degrees.
In large bowl, mix all ingredients together.
Drop little balls of mixture onto greased cookie sheet.
Bake for 15 to 20 minutes.

Makes 2 dozen cakes

Serve by candlelight and enjoy!

"When a man's best friend is his dog, that dog has a problem."
- Edward Abbey

Question:

Where do dogs come from?

Answer:

Dogs probably descended from an animal called Tomarctus. This animal lived around 15 million years ago.

CHEESE & GARLICK WOOF TREATS

1 1/2 c. whole wheat flour
1 1/4 c. cheddar cheese (grated)
1/2 c. corn oil margarine (softened)
1 clove garlic, crushed
Pinch of salt
Low fat milk

Preheat oven to 375 degrees.
Grate the cheese and let stand until it reaches room temperature. Mix the margarine, garlic, salt, cheese and flour together. Add milk until a ball forms. Chill for 1 hour. Roll onto floured surface. Using a cookie cutter, cut into little treats. Bake for 20 minutes.

Makes 3 dozen treats

Excellent with a side of salt-free crackers!

"Rambunctious, rumbustious, delinquent dogs become angelic when sitting."

- Dr. Ian Dunbar

Trivia Time...

Stone-aged people tamed dogs to help them hunt. Around 8,000 years ago, ancient Egyptians raised Saluki hunting dogs. Saluki means "noble one" in Arabic. These dogs are probably the oldest known breed.

MESQUITE BASTED BBQ BISCUITS

1 c. whole wheat flour
1 c. all purpose flour
1/2 c. nonfat dry milk powder
1/2 c. wheat germ
1/4 tsp. salt
6 tbsp. shortening
1 egg, slightly beaten
1 tsp. brown sugar
1/2 c. cold water
mesquite BBQ sauce

Preheat oven to 325 degrees.
Mix dry ingredients and then blend in shortening.
Blend the dry mixture with the egg, brown sugar and water.
Knead for 5 minutes.
Roll dough out to 1/2 inch thick. Shape into biscuits.
Bake for 30 minutes.
When cool, brush with BBQ sauce, return to preheated 350 degree oven, and bake for another 7 minutes.

Makes about 40 tasty biscuits

Brings home the flavor of summer camp!

"The old saw about old dogs and new tricks only applies to certain people."

- Daniel Pinkwater
'Train Your Dog, Dammit!'

Trivia Time...

"Argos," the dog belonging to Ulysses, was the only one who recognized the Greek hero when he came home, disguised as a beggar, after 20 years of adventure.

YOUR BASIC BISCUITS

4 c. all purpose flour
3 c. oatmeal
4 tbsp. oil
1 egg
2 tbsp. brown sugar
2 c. water
1 beef bouillon cube

Preheat oven to 300 degrees.
Mix ingredients together.
Shape into a basic biscuit.
Place on greased cookie sheet.
Bake for 55 minutes.
Allow to cool.

Makes 48 biscuits

Best served with a sprig of parsley and a bowl of chilled water!

"I talk to him when I'm lonesome like, and I'm sure he understands. When he looks at me so attentively, and gently licks my hands; Then he rubs his nose on my tailored clothes, but I never say naught thereat, For the good Lord knows I can buy more clothes, but never a friend like that!"

- W. Dayton Wedgefarth

Trivia Time...

The world's first space traveler was a dog named Laika, launched from Russia in 1957.

ALMOND MADNESS BISCUITS

1 c. whole wheat flour
1/2 c. wheat germ
1/2 c. nonfat dry milk powder
1/4 tsp. salt
1/4 c. sliced almonds
6 tbsp. shortening
4 drops almond oil
1 tsp. brown sugar
1 egg
1/2 c. water

Preheat oven to 325 degrees.
Combine flour, wheat germ, dry milk, salt and almonds.
Blend in the shortening and almond oil.
Beat brown sugar, egg and 1/4 cup of the water - add remaining water and mix with other ingredients.
Knead until smooth. Roll 1/2 inch thick, and shape into biscuits.
Bake for 30 minutes.

Makes 36 biscuits

Crunchy... munchy... tasty fun!

"The Dachshund's affectionate. He wants to wed with you: Lie down to sleep, And he's in bed with you. Sit in a chair, He's there. Depart, You break his heart."

- E. B. White

Question:

What was the name of the three-headed dog who guarded the gates to the underworld, according to Greek mythology?

Hint: It wasn't "Fido"

Answer:

Cerberus

MAPLE FLAVORED TAIL-WAGGIN' WONDERS

4 c. all purpose flour
1 c. oatmeal
1 tsp. imitation maple flavoring
1/3 c. vegetable oil
4 vegetable bouillon cubes
1 1/2 c. water

Preheat oven to 300 degrees.
Dissolve bouillon in water.
Mix all ingredients.
Roll out 1/2 inch thick.
Shape into biscuits.
Bake for 25 minutes.

Makes 36 tail-waggin' wonders

"Tell me, if you can, of anything that's finer than an evening in camp with a rare old friend and a dog after one's heart."

- Nash Buckingham
Hail and Farewell

Trivia Time...

The African basenji is the only dog that cannot bark.

AWESOME ORANGE BISCUIT BITES

3 1/2 c. all purpose flour
2 c. whole wheat flour
1 c. rye flour
2 c. bulgur (cracked wheat)
1/2 c. nonfat dry milk powder
1 tsp. salt
1 pkg. active dry yeast
1/4 c. warm water
1 tbsp. milk
2 c. chicken stock
1/4 tsp. imitation orange flavoring
1 tsp. orange juice concentrate
1 egg (beaten)

Preheat oven to 300 degrees. Combine all dry ingredients. Dissolve yeast in 1/4 cup of warm water, then add to the chicken stock. Mix wet and dry ingredients with orange flavoring and juice concentrate. On floured surface, roll out to 1/4 inch thick - cut into cookies. Mix milk with egg and brush on cookies. Bake for 45 minutes & turn oven off. Leave in oven overnight.

Makes 48 cookies

Refreshing on warm summer nights!

"A dog is not 'almost human,' and I know of no greater insult to the canine race than to describe it as such."

- John Holmes

Question:

What is the largest dog?

Answer:

The Irish Wolfhound

BITS O' BURGLAR

(looks like burglar, tastes like chicken)

3 1/2 c. all purpose flour
2 c. whole wheat flour
1 c. rye flour
1 c. corn meal
2 c. cracked wheat
1/2 c. nonfat dry milk powder
1/2 tsp. salt
2 c. chicken stock
1 pkg. yeast
1/4 c. warm water
1 tbsp. milk
1/2 cup of jerky pieces

Preheat oven to 300 degrees.
Mix dry ingredients (except yeast).
Dissolve yeast in warm water.
Add dry mixture and mix well with chicken stock & jerky
Roll into 1/2 inch thickness on ungreased sheet.
Design & cut into the shape of burglar.
Brush with milk. Bake 45 minutes.
Turn off oven and leave in overnight.

Makes 36 burglar shaped treats

Watch your watchdog chomp 'em down!

"The usual dog about the town is much inclined to play the clown."

- T. S. Eliot

Question:

What are the three categories of barking?

Answer:

Recreational, territorial and separation-anxiety.

VEGETARIAN BOWSER BISCUITS

1 1/2 c. whole wheat flour
1 c. buckwheat flour
1/2 c. nonfat dry milk powder
1/2 tsp. salt
1/4 tsp. garlic powder
6 tbsp. margarine
1 egg
2 tsp. brown sugar
1 c. pureed vegetables
(celery, peas, carrots, etc.)
1/2 c. ice water

Preheat oven to 350 degrees.
Combine dry ingredients and cut in margarine until mixture resembles cornmeal. Blend in egg, sugar, vegetables, and enough water to make mixture form a ball.
Roll to 1/2" thick on a floured surface.
Cut with cookie cutter.
Arrange on greased cookie sheet.
Bake for 30 minutes. Allow to cool completely.

Makes about 12 biscuits

A healthy addition to any diet

"Generally, or at least very often,
people with a deep
interest in animals are the
best people around."

- Roger Caras
'A Dog Is Listening'

Trivia Time...

There are over 400 breeds of dogs.

BISCUITOLI ITALIANO

3 1/2 c. all purpose flour
2 c. whole wheat flour
1 c. corn meal
1 c. rye flour
2 c. cracked wheat
1/2 c. nonfat dry milk powder
1/2 tsp. garlic powder
1 tsp. salt
dash of thyme - pinch of basil -
shake of oregano
2 2/3 c. chicken broth
1 pkg. yeast
1/4 c. warm water

Preheat oven to 300 degrees.
Mix flours, garlic powder, thyme, basil, oregano, milk and salt together. Dissolve yeast in warm water. Add to dry ingredients with broth and stir until dough forms a ball. Roll 1/4 inch thick.
Cut into shapes of Italy. Bake 45 minutes.
Turn off oven and dry overnight.

Makes 35 to 40 biscuits.

A romantic treat to serve while playing soft music

"When an animal has feelings that are delicate and refined, and when they can be further perfected by education, then it becomes worthy of joining human society. To the highest degree the dog has all these qualities that merit human attention."

- Count of Buffon
Histoire Naturelle

Question:

Can you bathe a dog too often?

Answer:

Yes. If washed too often, a dog may develop dry skin and dand-ruff (really).

NUTRITION YUM-YUMS

3 1/2 c. all purpose flour
3 c. whole wheat flour
2 c. oatmeal
1 c. cornmeal
1/4 c. nonfat dry milk powder
1 tsp. salt
1 1/4 c. chopped mixed vegetables
(celery, carrots, peas)
1 clove garlic
2 c. boiling water
2 envelopes dry yeast blended
with 1/2 c. warm water
1 egg, mixed with 1 tbsp. milk

Preheat oven to 300 degrees.
In large bowl, mix dry ingredients.
Mix garlic and vegetables together, then boil in the water for 10 minutes.
Cool, then add to dry mixture with yeast mixture.
Mix well. Add more water if too stiff.
Roll dough to 1/4" thickness. Shape into biscuits.
Brush with milk and egg mixture.
Bake for 45 minutes.

Makes 12 dozen yummy yum-yums

Excellent for any health conscious canine

"I like them all - pointers, setters, retrievers, spaniels - what have you. I've had good ones and bad of several kinds. Most of the bad ones were my fault and most of the good ones would have been good under any circumstances."

- Gene Hill

Question:

How would you describe someone who is looking for something in the wrong place?

Answer:

You would say they are "barking up the wrong tree."

PRESERVATIVE FREE BISCUITS

2 c. whole wheat flour
1/4 c. cornmeal
1/4 c. wheat germ
1/4 c. nonfat milk
1 egg, beaten
1/4 c. chicken or beef broth
1 lg. clove garlic, minced
1 tbsp. margarine (softened)
1 tbsp. molasses

Preheat oven to 375 degrees.
Mix dry ingredients together.
Mix egg & broth in separate bowl.
Slowly blend both mixtures together.
Add garlic, molasses and margarine.
On floured surface, roll dough out to a thickness of 1/4 inch. Cut into fun shapes.
Place biscuits on cookie sheet. Bake 15 to 20 minutes.
Allow to cool completely.
May be frozen if not immediately used.

Makes 36 biscuits

WARNING: These will not last!

"Don't accept your dog's admiration as conclusive evidence that you are wonderful."

\- Ann Landers

Question:

What, in general, is the smallest species of dog?

Answer:

Chihuahua

CANINE COCONUT CRUNCHIES

2 c. whole wheat flour
2 tbsp. soy flour
2 tbsp. wheat germ
2 tbsp. nonfat dry milk powder
1/2 tsp. salt
2 eggs (beaten)
4 tbsp. water
1/4 c. shredded coconut
5 drops coconut oil

Preheat oven to 350 degrees.
Mix all ingredients together.
Roll out on floured surface and cut into
little crunchies 3/4" X 2 1/2".
Place 1 inch apart on ungreased cookie sheet.
Bake for 30 minutes.
Flip over and bake another 30 minutes.
Remove and cool on racks.

Makes 16 crunchies

Serve with fresh cut flowers!

"The nose of the bulldog has been slanted backwards so that he can breathe without letting go."

- Winston Churchill

Question:

What is the heaviest breed of dog?

Answer:

The Saint Bernard

BANANA BAKES

1/2 c. quick oats
1/2 c. corn meal
3/4 c. wheat germ
1 1/4 c. all purpose flour
1/4 tsp. salt
1/4 tsp. sugar
1/2 tsp. brewers yeast powder
1/4 c. vegetable oil
1 mashed banana
5 drops banana oil
1/4 c. chicken stock

Preheat oven to 350 degrees.
Mix above ingredients in a bowl until dough forms.
Roll out 1/2 inch thick on floured surface.
Cut into biscuit shapes.
Place on greased cookie sheet.
Bake 40 minutes, until golden brown.

Makes about 35 biscuits

Perfect on hot summer days by the pool!

"Qui me amat, amat et canem meum.
Love me, love my dog."

- St. Bernard De Clairvaux
'Sermo Primus' 1150

Trivia Time...

If you can hear a sound 25 yards away, then your dog can hear the same sound 250 yards away!

TURKEY TREATS

2 1/2 c. whole wheat flour
1/2 c. nonfat dry milk powder
1/2 c. cold water
1/4 c. minced turkey
1 tsp. sugar
2 tbsp. turkey gravy
1/2 tsp. salt
6 tbsp. margarine
1 egg

Preheat oven to 350 degrees.
Mix dry milk & water.
Mix all ingredients.
Knead for 3 minutes.
Roll 1/2 inch thick.
Cut into biscuit shapes and place on greased cookie sheet.
Bake for approximately 30 minutes.

Makes about 24 treats

Wonderful at Thanksgiving time!

"We never really own a dog as much as he owns us."

- Gene Hill

Trivia Time...

A dog's heart beats between 70 and 120 times a minute. A human heart beats between 70 and 80 times a minute.

GARLICK GLORY

4 c. whole wheat flour
2 eggs
1 c. broth, chicken, beef, etc.
1/4 tsp. garlic salt
1/8 tsp. crushed garlic
1/4 tsp. garlic powder
1 1/2 - 2 tsp. wheat germ

Preheat oven to 350 degrees.
Mix all the ingredients in large bowl.
Roll out onto floured surface and cut into little pieces.
Place pieces on greased cookie sheet and bake until hard.
Time varies according to size.

Makes approx. 24 biscuits

And you thought Bowser's breath was bad NOW!

"The dog has seldom been successful in pulling man up to its level of sagacity, but man has frequently dragged the dog down to his."

- James Thurber

Trivia Time...

A female dog carries her young about 60 days before the puppies are born.

MOLASSES CRUNCHIES

1 pkg. active dry yeast
1 c. warm chicken broth
4 tbsp. molasses
1 3/4 - 2 c. all purpose flour
1 1/2 c. whole wheat flour
1 2/3 c. cracked wheat
1/2 c. cornmeal
1/2 c. nonfat dry milk powder
1 1/2 tsp. garlic powder
1 tsp. salt
1 egg, mixed with 1 1/2 tbsp. milk

Preheat oven to 300 degrees.
Dissolve yeast in 1/4 cup warm water - stir in broth and molasses. Add 1 cup of the all purpose flour, plus all other ingredients (except egg & milk). On floured surface, knead in second cup of all purpose flour.
Roll out to 1/2 inch thick - cut into desired shapes.
Place on ungreased baking sheet, brush tops with beaten egg and milk mixture. Bake for 45 minutes.
Turn off oven and leave in for 24 hours.

Makes 42 to 48 biscuits

A nice change for Bowser's sweet-tooth!

"When a dog runs at you, whistle for him."
- Henry David Thoreau

Question:
What saying indicates an empty threat?

Answer:
"A barking dog never bites."
(at least as long as he's barking)

FRISBEE FUN CHEWS

3 c. all purpose flour
2 eggs
1 tsp. garlic salt
Water or bouillon broth

3 tbsp. beet juice
3 tbsp. carrot juice
3 tbsp. pineapple juice
3 tbsp. grape juice

Preheat oven to 350 degrees.
Mix first four ingredients together to make a stiff dough.
Divide dough into four parts.
Add a different juice to each part (for color & flavor).
- add food coloring if desired -
Mix each part well until color is evenly blended.
Roll out, cut into round frisbee-like circles using a drinking glass. Bake 15 to 20 minutes or until hard.

Makes about 24 frisbee chews

It's a snack... It's a toy!

"Barking dogs don't bite, but they themselves don't know it."

- Shalom Aleichem

Question:

How would you describe a person who keeps others from using something that he himself cannot use?

Answer:

You would call him a "dog in a manger."

MAILMAN MUNCHIES

1 c. whole wheat flour
1 c. all purpose flour
1/2 c. wheat germ
1 tsp. ginger
1 tsp. cinnamon
1 tsp. sugar
1/2 c. nonfat dry milk powder
1/2 tsp. salt
6 tbsp. bacon fat or shortening
1 egg, mixed with 1 tsp. brown sugar
1/2 c. water

Preheat oven to 325 degrees.
Mix first 8 ingredients in bowl.
Blend in bacon fat or shortening.
Add egg, sugar and water.
Knead for 5 minutes.
Roll out on floured board to 1/2 inch thick.
Cut in the shape of your local mail carrier.
Put on greased cookie sheets and bake 30 to 45 minutes.
For munchier munchies, leave in oven to cool.

Makes approx. 18 munchies

Satisfies your dog's instinctive desire, while saving your postal carrier's dignity!

"You didn't have to throw a stick in the water to get him to go in. Of course, he would bring back a stick to you if you did throw one in. He would even have brought back a piano if you had thrown one in."

- James Thurber

The Thurber Carnival

Question:

Which saying means to leave a situation undisturbed?

Answer:

"Let sleeping dogs lie."

K-9 KRUNCHIES

3 1/2 c. all purpose flour (approx.)
1 c. whole wheat flour
1/4 c. rye flour
1 c. cornmeal
1 c. cracked wheat (bulgur)
1/4 tsp. garlic powder
1 c. nonfat dry milk powder
1 tsp. salt
1/4 tsp. minced garlic
1 pkg. dry yeast, dissolved in
1/2 c. warmed chicken stock
1 egg, mixed with 1 tbsp. milk

Preheat oven to 300 degrees.
Mix the ingredients together. Knead 5 minutes.
Roll the dough 1/4 inch thick.
Brush with egg & milk mixture. Bake for 45 minutes.
Turn the heat off and leave in the oven for 24 hours.

Makes about 30 cookies

Extra crunchy for a sparkling smile!

"The bond with a true dog is as lasting as the ties of this earth can ever be."

- Konrad Lorenz
'Man Meets Dog'

Question:

Which saying means that a subversive member of a group is actually directing everyone's activities?

Answer:

"Tail wagging the dog."

TASTEBUD TANTALIZING TUNA TASTIES

2 c. all purpose flour
2 c. cornmeal
1 c. grated Parmesan cheese
drained oil from small can of tuna
canned tuna
1/2 c. water or broth

Preheat oven to 300 degrees.
Combine flour, cornmeal, and cheese in large bowl.
Blend in oil until mixture is crumbly.
Add water (or broth), add tuna and mix well.
Roll dough out on floured surface to 1/2 inch thick.
Cut into 2 inch biscuits.
Place on ungreased baking sheet.
Bake for 45 minutes.
Allow to cool completely.

Makes about 2 dozen tuna tasties

Fishing.. smishing... bring on the Tuna Tasties!

**"Dogs love company.
They place it first on
their short list of needs."**

- J.R. Ackerley
'My Dog Tulip'

Question:

**I follow my master, Orion,
as he makes his annual journey
through the sky. Who or what am I?**

Answer:

Canis Major - The Great Dog

BACON FLAVORED FIRE HYDRANT FUN COOKIES

2 1/2 c. whole wheat flour
1/2 c. nonfat dry milk powder
1/4 tsp. salt
1 tsp. brown sugar
1/2 tsp. garlic powder
6 tbsp. bacon drippings or shortening
1 egg, beaten
1/2 c. ice-cold water
bacon bits

Preheat oven to 350 degrees. Combine all dry ingredients. Blend in shortening. Mix in beaten egg - add cold water to form stiff dough. Add crushed bacon bits to taste. Roll out to 1/2 inch thick - shape into fire hydrants. Place on lightly greased cookie sheet. Bake 25 minutes.

Makes about 24 fire hydrant cookies

Bring home the bacon!

"Man is troubled by what might be called the Dog Wish, a strange and involved compulsion to be as happy and carefree as a dog."

- James Thurber
'And So To Medve'

Question:

I am located on the shoulder of Canis Major. And I am the brightest in the heavens. Also, my name means "sparkling and scorching," because I am nearest to the sun during the height of summer. Who or what am I?

Answer:

Sirius, also known as the *Dog Star.*

SINFUL CINNAMON SNARLS

2 c. whole wheat flour
1/2 c. cornmeal
2/3 c. water
6 tbsp. oil
1 egg
1 tsp. brown sugar
1 tsp. vanilla
2 tbsp. cinnamon

Preheat oven to 350 degrees.
Mix all together.
On floured surface, roll out to 1/4 inch thick.
Cut into little devil shapes.
Bake for 45 minutes.

Makes about 24 sinful devil biscuits

Serve as a candlight dinner (a nice Halloween treat)

"Try throwing a ball just once for a dog. It would be like eating only one peanut or potato chip. Try to ignore the importuning of a Golden Retriever who has brought you his tennis ball, the greatest treasure he possesses!"

- Roger Caras
'A Dog Is Listening'

Question:

Why do dogs have tails?

Answer:

For balance while running.

HAMBURGER TUM-TUM SQUARES

2 c. whole wheat flour
1 c. cornmeal
1/4 c. brewer's yeast powder
1/2 lb. hamburger
2 tsp. garlic powder
1/2 tsp. salt
2 egg yolks
3 beef bouillon cubes dissolved in 1 1/2 c. boiling water

Preheat oven to 375 degrees.
Mix all ingredients well.
On floured surface, roll to 1/2 inch thick.
Cut into little squares.
Bake for 20 minutes on ungreased cookie sheet.
Keep in refrigerator & use quickly or freeze.

Makes about 30 squares

Makes a wonderful addition to any picnic!

"Poodles always listen attentively while being scolded... looking innocent, bewildered, and misunderstood."

- James Thurber

Trivia Time...

Dogs do not need to chew food thoroughly in order to digest it. Eating fast and swallowing whole pieces are considered normal.

LOVE BISCUITS

1 pkg. active dry yeast
1/4 c. warm water
1 c. warm chicken broth
2 tbsp. molasses
dash of garlic powder
1 c.+ all purpose flour
1 3/4 to 2 c. whole wheat flour
1 c. cracked wheat (bulgur)
1/2 c. cornmeal
1/2 c. nonfat dry milk powder
1 1/2 tsp. crushed garlic
5 drops red food coloring
1 tsp. salt
dash of love

Preheat oven to 300 degrees.
Dissolve yeast in 1/4 cup warm water - stir in broth and molasses. Add 1 cup of the all-purpose flour, the whole wheat flour, garlic powder, cracked wheat, cornmeal, dry milk powder, garlic, red food coloring and salt. Mix well. On floured surface, knead in more flour until dough is stiff. Roll out to 1/2 inch thick. Cut into heart shaped biscuits. Place on ungreased baking sheets. Bake for 45 minutes. Turn off heat and leave overnight.

Makes about 48 heart shaped biscuits

Lovely with a glass of *whine!*

"Dogs are very different from cats in that they can be images of human virtue. They are like us."
- Iris Murdoch

Question:
What does it mean when a dog's tail is up high?

Answer:
That the dog is confident of something.

POOCH'S PRETZELS

1 1/2 tsp. brown sugar
2 tsp. active dry yeast
2/3 c. boiling water
3/4 c. whole wheat flour
3 tbsp. low fat soy flour
1/4 c. nonfat dry milk powder
1 tbsp. dried liver powder
1 tbsp. bone meal flour
1 tsp. salt
2 drops yellow food coloring
1/4 tsp. garlic powder
1 egg, beaten (1/2 in recipe, 1/2 in glaze)
2 tbsp. cooking oil

Preheat oven to 375 degrees. Dissolve yeast and sugar in warm water. Combine dry ingredients. Add half of the beaten egg, oil and yeast-water mixture. Mix well, then add yellow food coloring. On floured surface, knead until firm. Place in oiled bowl, cover and let rise until double in size. Shape into pretzels and place on greased cookie sheet. Bake in oven for 15 minutes. Remove and brush with egg (beaten). Return to oven and bake at 300 degrees for about 15 minutes.

Makes about 30 pretzels

Serve these at pooch's next party!

"If a dog will not come to you after having looked you in the face, you should go home and examine your conscience."

- Woodrow Wilson

Age Comparison Chart
for Dogs vs. Humans

Dog years	Human years
3 months	5 years
6 months	10 years
1 year	15 years
2 years	24 years
4 years	32 years
6 years	40 years
8 years	48 years
10 years	56 years
14 years	72 years
18 years	89-92 years
20 years	93-97 years
21 years	98-107 years

CARROT CRUNCHIES

4 c. whole wheat flour
2 eggs
1 c. broth, chicken, beef, etc.
1/4 tsp. garlic salt
1/2 c. chopped carrots
1/4 tsp. garlic powder
1 1/2 - 2 tsp. wheat germ

Preheat oven to 350 degrees.
Mix all the ingredients in large bowl.
Roll out onto floured surface and cut into little pieces.
Place pieces on greased cookie sheet
and bake until hard.
Time varies according to size.

Makes approx. 24 biscuits

Invite the neighborhood dogs for a party they'll never forget!

**"Even the tiniest
Poodle or Chihuahua
is still a Wolf at heart"**

- Dorothy Hinshaw Patent
'Dogs: The Wolf Within'

Trivia Time...

**A dog can determine certain smells
all the way down to one part in ten quadrillion.
(*One* quadrillion is a million billions)
So the ratio of what a dog can smell is:
1 in 10,000,000,000,000,000**

TROPICAL TREASURE

1 1/2 c. all purpose flour
1 egg
1/2 tsp. sugar
1/2 tsp. coconut (grated)
pineapple juice

Preheat oven to 350 degrees.
Mix the flour, sugar, egg,
coconut & pineapple juice together
to make a stiff dough. Roll out, cut into biscuits.
Bake 15 to 20 minutes.
Turn oven off and let cool overnight (in oven).

Makes 20 small biscuits

Cancel Fido's trip to Hawaii!
Bring the tropics home!

**"Heaven goes by favor.
If it went by merit, you would stay
out and your dog would go in."**

- Mark Twain

Question:

**How long ago was the first dog
domesticated by humans?**

Answer:

Around the end of the ice age.

Chilling, but true.

HONEY-VANILLA CANINE COOKIES

Two 2 1/2 ounce jars of chicken baby food (without onion powder).
2/3 c. wheat germ
1/2 tsp. vanilla
1 tsp. Honey
1 1/4 c. nonfat dry milk powder

Preheat oven to 350 degrees.
Mix all the above ingredients.
Drop rounded tablespoons of mixture onto a greased cookie sheet.
Press into cookies with a fork.
Bake for 13 minutes. Let stand until cool.

Makes 24 cookies

A lovely mid-afternoon snack!

"If a dog's prayers were answered, bones would rain from the sky."

- Proverb

Question:

How much of a dog's brain is used strictly for the sense of smell?

Answer:

1/8

PEANUT BUTTER BOWSER BISCUITS

1 2/3 c. whole wheat flour
1/2 c. soy flour
1/2 tsp. sugar
1 1/8 tbsp. baking powder
1/2 tsp. salt
1 c. peanut butter
3/4 c. milk

Preheat oven to 400 degrees.
Combine flours, baking powder, sugar and salt in bowl.
In another bowl, blend peanut butter and milk until smooth. By hand, blend both mixtures together.
Place mixture onto floured surface and knead.
Roll dough out to 1/4 inch thick. Shape and cut into squares.
Place 1 inch apart on ungreased baking sheets.
Bake 15 minutes or until lightly browned.

Makes 36 biscuits

Don't forget a tall glass of milk!

"Dog movies nowadays are not what dog movies were 50 or even 10 years ago. For one thing, the dogs have become better actors."

- Benjamin Cheever

Question:

How many more sensory cells (for smelling) does a dog have compared to a human?

Answer:

44 times more!

And that is nothing to sneeze at.

CARROT CAROB BIRTHDAY CAKE

a healthy alternative for your chocolate loving pooch!

6 c. whole wheat flour
1 c. wheat germ
5 c. oatmeal
pinch of salt - dash of sugar
2 tbsp. brown sugar
1/4 c. peanut oil
1/4 c. corn oil margarine
1 c. shredded carrots
1/2 c. molasses
2 c. water
1 c. nonfat dry milk powder
4 oz. Carob chips, melted

Preheat oven to 300 degrees.
In a large bowl, mix together dry ingredients (except powdered milk). Mix water & powdered milk separately, add to dry mix. Add remaining ingredients and blend until smooth. Refrigerate the mixture until cold. Roll onto a greased cookie pan and cut into pieces (1/2 inch thick). Punch hole for candle. Bake 1 hour. Allow to cool for one hour. Frost with melted carob.

Makes 4 - 6 dozen Happy Birthday Biscuit Cakes

Chocoholics rejoice!

"It's no coincidence that man's best friend cannot talk."

- Anonymous

Question:

How much did the heaviest dog weigh?

Answer:

343 lbs and was 8 feet 3 inches long. The dog's name was Zorba and this information was recorded in 1989.

SCRUMPTIOUS STRAWBERRY SNACKS

2 1/2 c. whole wheat flour
1/2 c. nonfat dry milk powder
1/2 tsp. each salt and garlic powder
1 tsp. brown sugar
6 tbsp. margarine
1 egg, beaten
1/4 tsp. strawberry oil
few drops red food coloring (as desired)
1/2 c. ice water

Preheat oven to 350 degrees.
Combine flour, dry milk, salt and sugar.
Cut in shortening and mix well.
Mix in egg, strawberry oil and food coloring.
Add water until mixture forms a ball.
Roll dough 1/2 inch thick.
Cut into little biscuits.
Bake 25-30 minutes.
Allow to cool.

Makes 36 biscuits

Garnish with slices of strawberry!

"Old dogs, like old shoes, are comfortable. They might be a bit out of shape and a little worn around the edges, but they fit well."

- Bonnie Wilcox
'Old Dogs, Old Friends'

Question:

How old was the world's oldest dog?

Answer:

Apparently his name was Bluey and he lived to be 29 1/2 years old.

MARVELOUS MAPLE MUNCHIES

2 c. whole wheat flour
1/4 c. white or yellow corn meal
1/4 c. wheat germ
1 lg. garlic clove, crushed
1/4 c. milk
1 egg
1/4 c. chicken or beef broth
1 tbsp. soft margarine
maple syrup

Preheat oven to 375 degrees.
In large bowl, mix dry ingredients together. Blend in all other ingredients, mix well. On floured surface, roll into a 1/4 inch sheet. Shape into biscuits. Bake on greased cookie sheet 15-20 minutes. When cool, brush with maple syrup, return to preheated 350 degree oven, and bake for another 7 minutes.

Makes 48 biscuits

"I can train any dog in five minutes. It's training the owner that takes longer."

- Barbara Woodhouse

Trivia Time...

A Labrador named "Snag," who works for U.S. Customs, has made $810,000,000.00 worth of drug seizures.

(good dog!)

"DO-IT-YOURSELF" BISCUIT KIT #1

aka ____________________ 'S CUSTOM JUICY CHOMPS
(your dog's name here)

(Choose the ingredients your dog prefers)

4 c. all purpose flour (white or wheat)
3 c. oatmeal (or granola)
4 tbsp. oil (corn or olive)
1 egg
2 tbsp. brown sugar (light or dark)
1 1/2 c. of ____________________
(your dog's favorite juice)

Preheat oven to 300 degrees.
Mix ingredients together.
Shape into biscuits.
Place on greased cookie sheet.
Bake for 55 minutes.
Allow to cool. For extra CRUNCHY biscuits,
turn oven off after 55 minutes, but leave in overnight!

Makes 48 biscuits

Every dog should be so lucky!

"The more I see of men, the better I like my dog."

- Frederick the Great

Trivia Time...

Over 66% of dog owners give their dog a gift for one or more major holidays.

"DO-IT-YOURSELF" BISCUIT KIT #2

aka CHEF ________________'S PERSONAL CHOICE

(your dog's name here)

4 c. all purpose flour
3 c. oatmeal
4 tbsp. oil
1 egg
2 tbsp. brown sugar
2 c. water
and ONE of the following :
3 tbsp. peanut butter - or -
3 tbsp. crushed garlic - or -
4 tbsp. minced chicken livers - or -
1/4 c. carob chips

Preheat oven to 300 degrees. Mix ingredients together. Shape into a basic biscuit. Place on greased cookie sheet. Bake for 55 minutes. Allow to cool.

Makes 48 biscuits

BONE APPÉTIT!

Doggie Demogrrraphics*

* Source: Pet Industry Joint Advisory Council, Washington DC, U.S.A.

Population:

U.S.A., 1990: 52.1 million dogs, in 35.1 million households, an average of 1.5 per household
U.S.A., 1996: 58.2 million dogs, in 36.4 million households, an average of 1.6 per household

Most Popular Breeds:

Labrador Retriever, Rotweiler, German Shepherd, Golden Retriever, Beagle, Poodle, Cocker Spaniel, Dachshund, Pomeranian, Yorkshire Terrier

Misc. (Industry):

Households with pets: 58 million (59%)
Number of Vets: 55,000
Number of pet stores: 10,500
Retail pet sales: $3.7 billion
Pet Industry overall sales: $21 billion
Retail dog/cat food sales: $9.4 billion

Misc. (Personal):

According to a recent survey:
Over 75% spend at least 4 hours a day with their dog.
Over 61% visit a groomer regularly.
Over 77% use veterinary prescription medications.
Over 98% visit a veterinarian regularly averaging over 4 visits per year.

Toll Free Phone Directory

: Insurance

ned Health Plan (Gainesville FL)	800-237-1255
stin Insurance (Justin TX)	800-972-0272
rkel Insurance (Glen Allen VA)	800-446-7925
lor Harris Insurance (The Plains VA)	800-291-4774
terinary Pet Insurance (Anaheim CA)	800-872-7387

t Identification

ntinental Kennel Club (US)	800-952-3376
tional Animal ID (Natchez MS)	800-647-6761
tional Dog Registry (Woodstock NY)	800-637-3647
t Protection Plus (Memphis TN)	800-238-7387
e Peace Corporation (Norfolk NE)	800-215-4760
Kennel Club Inc (Bellmore NY)	800-352-8752

t Cemeteries

nine Monument (Centerville IL)	800-900-1777
erished Memories (High Point NC)	800-884-8262
t Memorial Park (Cary IL)	800-683-9921
nver Pet Cemet. (Commerce City CO)	800-280-0177

sc. Pet Services

-Breed Grooming (Front Royal VA)	888-280-5603
imal Communications (Aloha OR)	800-730-7255
nine Pedigree Services (Glydon MN)	800-832-7010
eedom Fence (Keene NH)	800-828-9089
oomer Direct (Brockport NY)	800-551-9860
rty Animals Inc (Ringwood NJ)	800-567-2789

t Transportation

: Animal Inc (Tampa FL)	800-635-3448
wood's Pet Resorts (Buckley WA)	800-232-2932
nine Carriers (Darien CT)	800-243-9105
:Y Pet Products (Van Nuys CA)	800-354-9909
t-A-Pet (Westport CT)	888-538-2738

Pet Products & Gifts

A. V. Pharmaceuticals (Browntown WI)	800-325-7552
Angell Dog Genealogy (Mocksville NC)	800-468-0882
Body Gear For Pets (Petaluma CA)	800-699-4050
Buck-L-eash, Inc. (Clearwater FL)	800-975-3274
California Collars (Oceanside CA)	800-767-7387
Canine Creations (Loveland OH)	800-337-7301
Designer Products (Arlington TX)	800-469-9416
Foggy M. Dog Coats (New Market MD)	888-364-2628
Pet Safety Products (Byram NJ)	800-448-4256
Poocheroo Pet Carrier (San Jose CA)	800-622-3775
Shining Star Embroidery (Sherman CT)	800-344-6746
Thompsons Pet Pasta (Kansas City KS)	800-228-3738

Pet Training

Dog Management (West Point CA)	800-262-3647
SuperPuppy (Escondido CA)	800-342-7877
Teach Me Dog Video (Scappoose OR)	800-833-1913
You Train (Foxton CO)	800-968-8724

Emergency Numbers

Spay USA (Port Washington NY)	800-248-7729
AKC (Raleigh NC)	919-233-9767
Assoc. of Pet Dog Trainers (Davis CA)	800-738-3647
ASPCA Poison Control (Urbana IL)	800-548-2423
Humane Society (Washington DC)	202-452-1100
ASPCA (New York NY)	212-876-7700

Veterinarian:

Dr.____________________________

Tel:____________________________

Animal Hospital:

Dr.____________________________

Tel:____________________________

Notes:

list your dog's allergies, likes, dislikes, etc...